JOB TO JOB FLOWS AND THE BUSINESS CYCLE

by

Henry Hyatt *
U.S. Bureau of the Census

and

Erika McEntarfer *
U.S. Bureau of the Census

CES 12-04   March, 2012

Introduction

Business cycle changes in labor turnover are important because declines in the rate at which workers are reallocated across jobs impacts the efficiency of the labor market. Workers and firms learn about the quality of a given job match, rejecting poor job matches for better ones, increasing worker wages and improving labor productivity. Such job changes are an important component of earnings growth over a worker's career, and changes in the rate of labor reallocation have implications for both wages and productivity.[1] For workers displaced from jobs, earnings losses can be severe; the ability to transition to new employment without substantial earnings losses varies across industries, skill-levels, and geography.[2] Better identification of winners and losers from the expansion and contraction of different industries could potentially inform the design of public policy responses to economic downturns, increased foreign competition, and other labor market shocks.

Despite the economic importance of worker reallocation across firms, these flows represent a significant gap in the set of available economic statistics. Regularly produced statistical tabulations typically aggregate survey responses from households or businesses (or both) to generate estimates that can be produced using cross sectional data -- output, unemployment, and productivity, etc. Increasingly, statistical agencies now provide measures that rely on repeated observations of an entity: job creation, employment accessions and

---

[1] Several researchers have documented the importance of job change in career wage growth, particularly for young workers (e.g. Topel and Ward, 1992 , Keith and McWilliams, 1999).

[2] Jacobson, Lalonde and Sullivan (1993) documented persistent wage losses for displaced workers in Pennsylvania in the 1980s. An overview of the large body of subsequent research on displaced workers is provided in Fallick (1996). Job separators who switch industries experience more substantial earnings losses, as shown by Neal (1995) and Parent (2000), and more recent studies have associated a large portion of such losses to occupation changes, see Polateav and Robinson (2008) and Kambourov and Manovskii (2009). For related studies documenting the returns to job tenure, see for example Altonji and Shakotko (1987) and Topel (1991).

separations, for example. In this paper, we demonstrate how matched employer-employee data can be used to calculate the frequency and economic consequences of movements from one job to another – a phenomenon that is basically absent from regularly produced statistical data products -- which we call job-to-job flows.

The Census Bureau is in the process of developing a new set of national job-to-job flow statistics derived from the Longitudinal Employer-Household Dynamics (LEHD) infrastructure files.[3] By linking matched employer-employee data over time, the LEHD program currently provides data on employment separations and accessions, job creation and job destruction, earnings and employment. Expanding that set of statistics to include flows across jobs exploits the ability in the LEHD data to link separations and accessions across employers. Unlike other available survey data sources such as the Current Population Survey (CPS), the LEHD administrative data is of sufficient size to provide public use statistics on these flows at detailed industry and geography levels.

Using new pilot job-to-job flow microdata constructed from the LEHD data as part of this data initiative, we calculate the frequency of different types of job-to-job flows, along with associated earnings changes for the years 1998-2010. We document a sharp fall in the rate of job change in the Great Recession, and a somewhat smaller decline in the 2001 recession. These declines in job mobility are found within all age groups but are largest for young workers, who generally have the highest rates of job change. We find that earnings changes associated with job change are procyclical, with strong penalties for nonemployment that follow a similar cyclical pattern. Earnings changes for all types of job change are at a series low in the Great Recession, with greater penalties associated with nonemployment in this period.

---

[3] For detailed description of the LEHD data, see Abowd et al. (2009) and Abowd, Haltiwanger, and Lane (2004).

We also provide detailed statistics on job-to-job flows by detailed industry and movements into nonemployment. We demonstrate that about half of all movements from one job to another are movements within an industry, and that within-industry movements tend to be associated with modest earnings increases. When workers move from one industry to another, some destination industries, such as Manufacturing, tend to be associated with earnings increases, while others, such as Leisure & Hospitality, tend to be associated with earnings decreases. We also take a closer look at labor market adjustment in the Great Recession in four selected NAICS sectors: Construction, Manufacturing, Finance & Insurance, and Health Care & Social Assistance. We find a drop in flows across employers and an increase in the rate of industry change and earnings loss, with a higher rate of flows to lower-wage industries during the years of the most recent recession.

Lastly, we examine displaced workers in the Great Recession and find that earnings losses are concentrated among those who experienced nonemployment after displacement. Greater earnings losses in the Great Recession than the 2001 recession is largely due to the higher share of displaced workers experiencing nonemployment. We provide these results for three selected industries: Construction, Finance & Insurance, and Health Care & Social Assistance. We find that the earnings losses are greatest for those who separate from jobs in Construction, and the inter-industry differences in earnings losses are driven by differences in post-separation nonemployment.

Measuring Flows of Workers Between Firms

National estimates of worker flows directly from one employer to another were first derived by Fallick and Fleischman (2004). To demonstrate the importance of on the job search in labor markets, they exploit dependent interviewing techniques used in the CPS to estimate monthly rates of job change without intervening nonemployment. Fallick and Fleischman estimate that 2.6% of employed persons change employers each month, and that this rate fell in the 2001 recession. Bjelland et al. (2011) use the LEHD data to estimate direct employer-to-employer flows, similar to Fallick and Fleischman. Using this measure, they estimate a quarterly employer-to-employer flow rate of about 4% and a high rate of industry change, with almost half of job changes involving industry changes.

The CPS has several advantages for estimating flows of workers across employers. It is the primary source of the data on flows of workers across labor market states, so flows between jobs can be estimated jointly with flows to unemployment and flows out of the labor market. The CPS sample is representative of the entire civilian population and earnings and employment data are not limited to particular sectors, or to household heads only. However, the CPS also has several limitations for the purpose of estimating job-to-job flow statistics. The size of its sample, while large for a survey of households, remains small for estimating flows between detailed industries or within smaller geographic areas. The representativeness of the CPS is compromised by significant attrition, and the survey does not follow workers when they change residences. Also, the CPS follows individuals for only four consecutive months, so long employment histories cannot be constructed.

The LEHD data we use here offer several advantages as a source for estimates of job-to-job flows. First, the universe of the LEHD data is employment covered by the state unemployment insurance (UI) system. State unemployment insurance system coverage is broad and basically comparable from state to state. Over 95% of private employment is covered, as is state and local government employment. The density of data makes possible analysis of flows of workers across detailed industries, demographic groups, and even flows of workers following specific regional economic shocks. Unlike the CPS, workers in the LEHD data can be followed for years.

All results described in this paper use a pilot database of job-to-job flows derived from LEHD data for 1998-2010. These measures expand on those used in Bjelland et al. in several ways. First and most importantly, we expand the universe of worker flows to include flows between jobs that have an intervening nonemployment spell. Our job-to-job flows include direct employer-to-employer flows, flows to new jobs with an intervening nonemployment spell, and job separations for which we do not observe a subsequent job. Second, the LEHD frame has expanded sufficiently for us to construct job histories that follow workers across state boundaries. Nine states serve as the frame for our analysis: CA, FL, GA, IL, KS, MI, NV, NC, and ND. Specifically, the frame for our analysis is all workers who held at least one job in these nine states during this time period. We then construct national job histories for these workers so that flows from and to out of state jobs are included in their job history. Lastly, we restrict ourselves to flows between primary jobs only. We define a primary job separation as a separation from a job that is the largest source of earnings either in that quarter or the previous quarter. Primary job accessions are defined symmetrically. We then track flows between these primary jobs, distinguishing between flows that occur within the same quarter vs. subsequent quarters, and track potential nonemployment spells between jobs. We provide precise definitions of our job-to-job flow measures in the Appendix of this paper.

Quarterly earnings data have several limitations which readers should keep in mind. First, in the administrative data we cannot distinguish between those who are unemployed and those not in the labor force. Furthermore, quarterly wage data does not provide exact start and end dates for jobs, so nonemployment durations are only approximately observed in quarterly earnings data. For example, a worker with one full quarter of nonemployment between jobs has nonemployment spell of three to eight months. This data frame also implies that the interesting category of "direct" job-to-job flows, that is, flows in which there is no intervening nonemployment, is a subset of the two categories of flows in which there is not a full quarter of nonemployment: flows in which the accession and separation are in the same quarter, as well as those in which the quarter of the accession immediately follows the quarter of separation. Note furthermore that to calculate earnings changes, we limit analysis to the subset of flows in which the transitions where workers move from a job that they hold for at least three consecutive quarters in both the origin and destination jobs, and consider earnings in the so-defined middle quarter: the latest "full quarter" available for the separation as well as the earliest "full quarter" for the accession, and to avoid considerations of outliers, we evaluate all earnings transitions from one job to another at the median.

Trends in Aggregate Job-to-Job Flows, 1998-2010

Figures 1 and 2 show seasonally adjusted primary job separations along with job-to-job and job-to-nonemployment-to-job flows in our database from 1998-2010. Separations are modestly procyclical, with a precipitous decline in the Great Recession. Job-to-job flows occurring within the same quarter and those where the new job began in the subsequent quarter demonstrate very similar cyclical patterns, and so are combined in Figures 1 and 2.

Figure 1 demonstrates several interesting facts about job-to-job flows and their relation to worker flows generally. First, job-to-job flows involving little or no nonemployment are procyclical, while job-to-nonemployment-to-job spells that involve at least one full quarter of nonemployment demonstrate either no cyclical pattern or in the case of those involving longer nonemployment spells, a countercyclical pattern. Thus the procyclicality of dominant job separations appears to be driven entirely by those first two types of job flows.[4] These two types of flows begin to fall in early 2007, preceding the official start of the Great Recession by a quarter or two and drop to a series (12-year) low by early 2009. The spike in separations to nonemployment spells of two or more quarters in late 2008 is driven almost entirely by a spike in separations to nonemployment spells lasting one year or more (not shown), consistent with the persistently high unemployment rate and long unemployment durations during this recession.

In Figure 2, worker flows are scaled to represent the quarterly frequency with which workers separate from their respective primary jobs. As in Figure 1, the decline in job mobility from 1998 to 2010 is substantial; the quarterly primary job separation rate falls from a peak of 18% in 2000 to 11% in 2010. The frequency with which workers change their primary job between one quarter and the next (the combined direct and adjacent quarter job-to-job flows) similarly declines by almost half in this same period, from a peak of 10.5% in 2000 to 5.5% in 2010. Together, these results suggest a substantial downward trend in job mobility throughout the last decade, driven by significant declines in rates of job change in both recessions.

What could be driving steep declines in job mobility in recessions? A straightforward explanation might be business cycle fluctuations in net job creation; fewer new jobs are created in recessions, and the resulting decline in hires limits job mobility for the already employed. Lazear and Spletzer (2012), however, find that 80% of the decline in hiring in from 2007 to 2009 was due to a decline in churn – hiring that simply fills vacancies left by departing employees without any addition to net job growth. Only 20% of the decline in hiring was due to a decline in

---

[4] A known shortcoming of the LEHD data is the inability to identify which job separations are quits vs. layoffs. The procyclical nature of job separations to new employment (in the current or subsequent quarter) suggests these separation types are dominated by quits.

job creation. Looking at trends in churn from 2001-2010, they find a procyclical trend in churn similar to the pattern we see for job flows to new employment in Figures 1 and 2. Together these suggest that the fall in job mobility in recessions is driven at least in part by employed workers being unwilling to separate from their current jobs in recessions. Workers may be less willing to take a risk on a new job in a period of high unemployment, reducing the flow of workers across firms in bad economic times.[5]

While risk-aversion on the part of workers may well explain the fall in job mobility in recessions, we also find evidence of a downward trend in job mobility generally during 1998-2010. The recovery in job mobility between recessions is quite weak in the LEHD data (this is particularly striking in Figure 2, which shows rates of job change), with job mobility in 2006 (the peak of the recovery period) still two percentage points lower than the earlier peak in 1999. To investigate the possibility that the general downward decline is due changing worker demographics (the aging of the workforce, and declining labor force participation rates of younger worker who change jobs more frequently), Figure 3 breaks out job-to-job flow rates by age group. As shown in Figure 3, job mobility declines within all age groups, with the sharpest absolute declines in job mobility in this period among younger workers, particularly those under 30. Over 15% of workers age 21-30 in 2000 change primary employers from one quarter to the next, compared to only 8.8% in 2010. Workers under 21 years of age decline from a peak rate of job change of 19.2% in 2000 to 10% in 2010.[6]

---

[5] Lazear and Spletzer (2012) also find evidence that employers are not filling vacancies as quickly in recessions. This too, however, could be the result of workers being less willing to leave existing jobs. Assuming that the most qualified candidates for any position are already employed, the quality of a pool of applicants for a vacancy will be lower in recessions. Thus the reduced willingness of workers to leave jobs might be driving the 'skills gap' frequently cited by employers as a cause of failure to fill vacancies.

[6] We also calculated rates of job change within sex * education * age groups to see if changing gender or education composition within young cohorts of workers could be driving the fall in rates of job change among young workers.

This suggests factors other than changes in worker demographics are driving the overall downward trend in job mobility. The very steep declines in job change in both recessions also suggest that reduced churn in recessions impacts younger workers most severely. This implies that focus on unemployment rates among the young capture only part of the effect of recessions on younger workers – many employed young workers are holding on to poor job matches much longer than they would in better economic times. As job change is an important contributor to wage growth for younger workers, the steep declines in job turnover for the young in recessions and the general downward decline in job mobility is a worrisome trend. To demonstrate the wide disparity in earnings gains for the young relative to older workers, Figure 4 shows smoothed seasonally adjusted median earnings changes from direct job-to-job (within-quarter) flows by age group. Earnings gains from job change for workers under 30 are much larger than for older workers, with workers aged 21-30 experiencing a median earnings gain from job change of 12%-16%, while workers aged 41-55 have a range of earnings growth of 2-5%. Interestingly, there is some evidence of recovery in earnings gains for workers in their twenties (even stronger for workers in their teens), but there is no evidence of recovery for other age groups.

So far, we have focused on trends in job flows and earnings change for job turnover with minimal nonemployment. Figure 5 compares earnings changes for direct flows to new jobs versus those flows with an intervening nonemployment spell. We find that earnings changes associated with job change decrease with both the presence and duration of a nonemployment spell between jobs, and that earnings changes associated with all types of flows have similar cyclical patterns. For example, in the second quarter of 2006, workers with direct job-to-job

---

While the levels of job change differed among the groups, the pattern of steep declines in mobility in both recessions is observed in each sex by education group over the 12 year panel.

flows experienced a 9% earnings gain, those with flows to a new job starting in the following quarter experience a 3.8% earnings gain, while those with one or two-three quarters nonemployment experience a 0% and -1.2% earnings change, respectively. What is perhaps most interesting in Figure 5 is the procyclical co-movement of earnings changes associated with most types of job flows. There is also some evidence here of an increased penalty for nonemployment in the Great Recession, while earnings gains for direct job-to-job flows are similar to the last recession, earnings losses are greater for those with 2-3 quarters of nonemployment.

Job-to-Job Flows by Industry

In this section, we present a description of the frequency of job-to-job flows by origin and destination industry, the frequency and duration of intervening nonemployment, and associated wage changes during the years 1999-2009. Industries are defined at the NAICS supersector level, and wage changes evaluated at the median. The results described here expand the analysis of job-to-job flows by origin and destination industry that appears in Bjelland et al. (2011), although readers should note that they consider different employer-to-employer flows: for example, they omit flows that involve a spell of nonemployment, and they consider only flows involving two quarters of continuous employment at both the employer of accession and separation.

The number of job-to-job flows that originate from employment and have a destination employer is listed by origin NAICS supersector in Table 1. The supersectors that originate the most job-to-job flows are Trade, Transportation and Utilities and Professional and Business Services, with more than 20 million each, followed by Leisure and Hospitality with more than 15 million and Education and Health Care with 12.4 million. Construction and Manufacturing each account for about 7 million flows, while the Financial Activites supersector accounts for five million. Smaller numbers of flows originate with Other Services (excluding Public Administration), with about 3 million flows, Natural Resources and Mining, with more than 2 million flows, and Public Administration with about 1.6 million flows.

Table 1 also shows the frequency of movement within and between NAICS supersectors, for all job-to-job flows involving a separation that occurred between 1999 and 2009 (subsequent accessions could occur during 2010). As previously noted in Bjelland et al. (2011), for each origin supersector, the most frequent destination supersector is in the same supersector, which generally accounts for somewhat less than half of all flows. Supersectors with more job-to-job flows tend to have proportionately more flows into the same supersector, with the exception of Natural Resources and Mining, a relatively small supersector in which more than half of all flows are to another job in the same supersector. The two supersectors that originate most job-to-job flows are consistently among the most frequent destination supersector: for most origin supersectors, 12%-15% of job-to-job flows are movements into Professional and Business Services and 9-16% are movements into Trade, Transportation and Utilities. Supersectors that originate fewer flows tend to be less frequent destinations.

Table 2 shows the median wage changes associated with flows from one supersector to another. Most flows with an origin and destination supersector tend to be associated with earnings increases. Origin supersectors that are associated with greater earnings increases are the destination supersectors with lower earnings increases. This is especially pronounced in the Leisure and Hospitality supersector, in which earnings decrease for more than half of all origin supersectors, and destination supersectors for job-to-job flows originating with the Leisure and Hospitality industry are with few exceptions associated with wage increases in excess of 30%.

Five supersectors, Natural Resources and Mining, Construction, Manufacturing, Information and Financial Activities have similar wage patterns: they tend to have small (single-digit) increases when an origin supersector, but have rather larger (double-digit) increases as a destination.

Table 3 shows the frequency of different job-to-job flow nonemployment types by origin supersector. Levels are rather different between industries, but, broadly, most industries have around one-quarter within-quarter flows, one-quarter adjacent-quarter flows, and then fewer in longer nonemployment categories. A few percent within each supersector are dominant employer flows in which there is not a distinct separation and accession, that is, a continuing job becomes a secondary or main job. Supersectors such as Financial Activities, Trade Transportation and Utilities and Professional and Business Services tend to have less nonemployment (25-28% are within-quarter job-to-job flows), while others have more nonemployment: for example, Natural Resources and Mining (only 17.6% within-quarter flows) and Public Administration (19% within-quarter flows).

Inter-industry differences in nonemployment rates are further explored in Table 4, which shows the fraction of separations from dominant employment that involve no intervening spell of nonemployment. Results are shown by year in order to assess how these measures changed during the expansion of 2000-2007, as well as during the preceding and subsequent recessions. Overall, like unemployment, nonemployment is counter-cyclical and its peaks lag the business cycle troughs. The frequency with which separations involve nonemployment increases from 1999-2003, then declines until 2006, at which point it surges. Separation to nonemployment is most frequent during the so-called "jobless recovery" and during the Great Recession of 2007: most industries have their highest rates of nonemployment in 2003 and 2009. The largest changes are associated with the Great Recession, when certain industries experienced sharp increases in nonemployment, with the largest increases from 2007-2009 occurring in Manufacturing (10 percentage points) and Construction (7 percentage points). Most industries experienced their lowest rates of nonemployment in 2006 or an adjacent year, with the exception of the Information and Financial Activities supersectors, which have marginally lower nonemployment in 2000 than 2006.

Analogous results on industry switching are shown in Table 6, which presents the frequency with which separations that do not involve nonemployment are to another job in the same industry. Recall from the discussion above that supersectors with more job-to-job flows also tend to have a higher share of job-to-job flows to other jobs within the same supersector. Industry switching appears to be procyclical: most industries have a local maximum in within-industry movement in the year 2003 or an adjacent year, and all but three industries have a global maximum in the year 2009. The three exceptions are Construction, Manufacturing and Public Administration, in which industry switching increases. Of these, Construction and Manufacturing, the two industries that exhibited the most significant contractions, have their lowest levels of within-industry movement in 2009: most other industries exhibit their lowest rate of within-industry switching in the year 2000.

Wage changes associated with separations from different supersectors are shown in Table 7, which lists the median wage change associated with any movement from full-quarter employment to full-quarter employment and may involve a spell of nonemployment, the same definition used in Table 2 above. Separations from the Leisure and Hospitality supersector are associated with strong wage gains throughout the cycle, while those from Professional and Business Services are the second-largest. Separations from Manufacturing are associated with wage declines in all years except 1999. Wage increases are pro-cyclical: most industries experience a decline in wages when switching jobs in 2009, and all supersectors exhibit their lowest change in the year 2008 or 2009. Most supersectors exhibit a local minimum in wage changes in 2002 or 2003.

Labor Market Adjustment for Selected Industries Before and During the Great Recession

One of the most interesting applications of a job-to-job flows series is the examination of how the labor force associated with a particular industry adjusts to a demand shock. In this section we examine four selected industries which received considerable attention during and after the Great Recession: Construction, Manufacturing, Finance & Insurance and Health Care & Social Assistance. The three former industries exhibited sharp declines in employment during the recession, while Health Care & Social Assistance did not. Of the contracting industries, Construction exhibited the earliest and most severe contraction, beginning with the collapse of the housing market in 2006.[7] Manufacturing employment contracted sharply during the recession years, although it had been decreasing for much of the preceding decade. In this section, we show the frequency of different nonemployment spells, as well as the wage changes associated with them. We provide statistics for three three-year time periods: 2001-2003, which includes the 2001 recession and the jobless recovery, the 2004-2006 period, when US output and employment were increasing, and 2007-2009, the years in which the US economy was in the recession of 2007. Earnings changes are calculated for the subset of job flows where the origin and destination jobs both involve a full quarter's work.

In Table 8, we present results on job-to-job flows by subsequent nonemployment for all spells that involve a separation along with an accession in a concurrent or subsequent quarter, or

---

[7] In Hyatt and McEntarfer (2011), we present a similar analysis for the residential construction industry.

nonemployment in the quarter that follows the separation.[8] For all four industries, around half of separations involve no full quarter nonemployment, and this fraction is highest during the expansion years of 2004-2006. From 2001-2003 to 2004-2006, the frequency of flows without full quarter nonemployment increases by 2 to 4 percentage points, and between 2004-2006 and 2007-2009 decreases by 2.4 (Health Care & Social Assistance) to 7.7 (Manufacturing) percentage points. Most of this change is associated with a decrease in those flows where the accession and separation occur in the same quarter. For each of the four selected industries, most the decrease in direct job-to-job flows can be accounted for by an increase in the frequency of non-employment that last for four or more quarters. For Construction separators, a 5.0 percentage point decline in direct job to job flows corresponds with a 3.8 percentage point increase in separations to non-employment that lasts for four or more quarters, for Manufacturing separators, a 7.7 percentage point decrease is associated with a 5.9 percentage point increase, for Finance & Insurance separators, a 4.2 percentage point increase is associated with a 4 percentage point increase, and for Health Care & Social Assistance separators, a 2.4 percentage point decrease in direct job-to-job flows corresponds with a 3.2 percentage point increase in separations to non-employment that lasts four or more quarters.

Earnings changes associated with job-to-job flows decline for all four industries during the recession years 2007-2009, when the duration of nonemployment also increased. Nonemployment is generally associated with earnings losses, and longer durations are associated with larger earnings losses. Median wage changes tend to decrease with nonemployment duration: the only exception in Table 8 is that wage declines are sometimes slightly larger for flows where separation occurs in the quarter immediately preceding accession, compared with

---

[8] This implies that flows in which an employment separation results in a continuing job becoming a main job or an accession in which a continuing (previously dominant) job becomes a secondary job are omitted.

those that have a full quarter of nonemployment, and this is most apparent for separators from Manufacturing. Earnings changes are lowest in the recession years. Median earnings changes for those flows in which the separation and accession occur in the same quarter are always positive, while separations assocated with non-employment of two or three quarters is always associated with wage declines at the median.

In Table 9, we present employment and earnings outcomes by industry for the subset of separators who experienced less than a full quarter of nonemployment, that is, either a within-quarter job-to-job flow or an adjacent-quarter flow. Within-sector reallocation decreased as a share of within-quarter and adjacent-quarter job-to-job flows in the three contracting industry sectors but not in Health Care. Construction shows an increase in flows to the low-wage Accommodation & Food Service sector, and at the median earnings decline sharply for such job flows. Movements into lower wage sectors are not as noticeable for other origin industries. Earnings gains associated with job change decline markedly in the Great Recession. Within-industry movements tend to be associated with small wage gains (see bolded lines of Table 9).

For Construction separators, relative to the 2004-2006 period, in 2007-2009, job-to-job flows decline to about 82% of their previous level, and conditional on taking place, nearly half of flows are to destinations outside construction. In recession years, there is decline in median earnings changes across destination sectors. In addition to this change, there is a more modest change in earnings due to the result of moves to low-wage sectors: among all NAICS sectors, the largest increase between 2004-2006 and 2007-2009 is a more than one percentage point increase in the share of flows into the Accommodation & Food Services sector, which are associated with large (16%-25%) downward movements in earnings. During the recession years, there is also an increase in movement to the Agriculture, Forestry, Fishing & Hunting which is associated with smaller (4%-10%) wage declines, as well as to Wholesale Trade, which is associated with modest (4%-8%) wage increases.

Throughout 2001-2009, the number of job-to-job flows that are movements within Manufacturing (Table 9b) are low relative to other industries (26%-29%), and they decline by two percentage points from 2004-2006 to the recession years. Almost half of this is accounted for by a less than one percentage point increase in flows to the Accommodation & Food Services sector, which is associated with substantial (24%-31%) declines in earnings. Other sectors that show substantial increases are Agriculture, Forestry, Fishing & Hunting and Health Care & Social Assistance, which are associated with smaller declines, as well as Professional, Scientific & Technical Services, which are associated with modest (1%-6%) earnings increases.

For job-to-job flows originating in Finance & Insurance (Table 9c), within-sector reallocations are highest in the expansion years of 2004-2006, and they decline by more than two percentage points to the recession years of 2007-2009, having exhibited a similarly-sized (but opposite sign) increase from 2001-2003 to 2004-2006. From the expansion to the recession years, the largest increase in reallocations is a 0.8 percentage point increase in flows to Health Care & Social Assistance, which follows a similar 0.8 percentage point decrease from 2001-2003 to 2004-2006. Movements from Finance & Insurance to Health Care & Social Assistance are associated with very little (-1% to +2%) change in earnings. Education Services and Professional, Scientific & Technical Services also exhibited substantial increases in the rate at which they appear as destination industries for flows originating in the Finance & Insurance sectors, and those flows are associated with declines and increases in earnings, respectively.

The Health Care & Social Assistance sector (Table 9d) exhibits an increase in the share of reallocations that are within-industry by more than two percentage points in the recession years. This gain is mostly accounted for by decreases in movements Administrative, Support & Waste Management, which is associated with modest (1%-2%) increases in earnings prior the years of the Great Recession, and associated with a small (1%) decrease during those years, as well as to Retail Trade, which is in the recession years associated with modest (5.5%) wage decrease, and to Manufacturing, which is associated with substantial (18%-23%) earnings increases.

Consequences of Job Loss in the Great Recession

The severe weakening of the labor market in the Great Recession lead to a correspondingly high rate of job loss, see Farber (2011). In this section we focus specifically on those workers who lost their jobs when their employers downsized (or closed) in the first two years of the recession. We identify job loss here in a manner similar to other displaced worker analysis using administrative data, especially Jacobson, LaLonde, and Sullivan (1993), by identifying firms that experienced a 30% or larger decline in employment in 2007 or 2008 relative to the firm's peak employment in the period 2004-2006. To be more comparable with that literature we further restrict our analysis here to prime age men (age 35-55) who had at least one year of tenure in the job prior to displacement. Note that in this section, for comparability with the existing literature, earnings changes in this section are not calculated for particular jobs, evaluated at the mean rather than the median, and are calculated for all workers rather than the subset in which full-quarter earnings are observed for a particular origin and destination job.

Figure 6 shows real total quarterly earnings changes after job loss for displaced prime age men in the Great Recession, conditional on re-employment, by presence of a nonemployment spell. For comparison purposes, we also show earnings changes upon re-employment for a group of displaced workers from the 2001 recession. Earnings losses for displaced workers are concentrated among those who experience at least one full-quarter of nonemployment (-20% quarterly earnings change eight quarters after job loss, compared to 0.2% among those reemployed the quarter following displacement). Conditional on re-employment, displaced workers in the Great Recession do not experience appreciably worse earnings outcomes than in the milder 2001 recession, with earnings losses quite close between the two groups (usually within 1-3 percentage points across the quarters). Figure 7, however, shows that displaced workers in the Great Recession are much more likely to experience at least one full-quarter of nonemployment (38.5% of displaced workers in the Great Recession, compared to 31.8% in the earlier recession). Eight quarters after job loss, 30% of displaced workers in the Great Recession still have zero earnings, compared to 23% in the 2001 recession.

The fate of unemployed construction workers in the Great Recession has been examined by several researchers recently, with somewhat contradictory conclusions. In a blog post for New York Federal Reserve, Crump and Sahin (2012) examine outcomes for unemployed construction workers and observe that, according to several indicators, construction workers are doing the same or better than unemployed workers in other sectors. Using data from the Displaced Worker Survey, they find evidence that displaced construction workers who are reemployed have the same distribution of earnings as other displaced workers who find a job. Fang and Silos (2012) respond using panel data from the SIPP; they examine wage changes for unemployed construction workers who change industries and find large earnings losses among these workers, larger than for other unemployed industry switchers, painting a more pessimistic (although not inconsistent) view of labor market adjustment for construction workers.

In Figure 8, we show how displaced construction workers in the LEHD data faired in the

Great Recession relative to workers in other selected industries. These results can be compared to earnings outcomes for all displaced workers shown in Figure 6. Displaced construction workers have much worse outcomes than displaced workers in finance and health care, with 5-6% earnings losses for construction workers who experience no nonemployment. Earnings losses are most severe and sustained among the nonemployed group, with displaced construction workers having 25% earnings losses eight quarters after job loss. Displaced construction workers experience larger earnings losses than displaced workers generally. Figure 9 shows nonemployment rates for the same set of industries; displaced construction workers have the lowest reemployment rate, with 40% experiencing at least a full quarter of nonemployment. Joblessness rates are also higher for construction workers than for displaced workers in all industries, shown in Figure 7.

Conclusion

This paper has two goals. Our first goal is to develop a pilot database of job-to-job flows from the LEHD data, as part of an initiative at Census to produce these flows as a new public use data product. Our second goal is to demonstrate the usefulness of such statistics by examining their trends over the business cycle, the corresponding earnings changes from job change, and the dynamics of worker flows across industries. While this analysis is descriptive and exploratory, we uncover some previously unknown (to the best of our knowledge) trends in labor market dynamics over the last 12 years.

We show evidence that the rate of job change has declined markedly over the last 12 years, driven by declines in both the 2001 recession and the Great Recession, with little evidence of a recovery in the intervening expansion. The aging of the workforce is rejected as a possible cause of this decline in labor turnover. Indeed, this decline is driven largely by steep falls in the rate of job change among young workers (particularly those under 30) which fall by almost half over this time period. We find evidence that wage gains from job change (as well as earnings losses associated with nonemployment) have a strong cyclical pattern. Comparing displaced workers across the two recessions, we find that conditional on re-employment, displaced workers do not fair comparably worse in the Great Recession compared to previous recessions (reemployment rates, however, are much lower in the more recent recession, consistent with the high and persistent unemployment rate in this period).

We observe high rates of industry change associated with job change and a good deal of heterogeneity in wage changes associated with different industry-industry flows (the highest wage increases are exits from leisure and hospitality, the greatest wage losses are flows from manufacturing or construction to leisure and hospitality). Comparing selected industries in depth, we find much stronger wage penalties associated with nonemployment in manufacturing, finance, and construction, compared to health care. We also find stronger wage penalties on reemployment for workers in construction and finance in the Great Recession compared to earlier periods.

REFERENCES

Abowd, John M. Haltiwanger, John C., and Lane, Julia I., 2004. "Integrated Longitudinal Employee-Employer Data for the United States", *American Economic Review Papers and Proceedings*, 94(2): 224-229.

Abowd, John M., Bryce E. Stephens, Lars Vilhuber, Fredrik Andersson, Kevin L. McKinney, Marc Roemer, and Simon D. Woodcock. 2009. "The LEHD Infrastructure Files and the Creation of the Quarterly Workforce Indicators." In *Producer Dynamics: New Evidence from Micro Data*, Vol. 68, Studies in Income and Wealth, ed. Timothy Dunne, J.Bradford Jensen and Mark J. Roberts, 149-230. Chicago: University of Chicago Press.

Altonji, Joseph and Robert Shakotko. 1987. "Do Wages Rise with Job Seniority?" *Review of Economic Studies*, 54(3): 437-459.

Bjelland, Melissa, Bruce Fallick, John Haltiwanger and Erika McEntarfer. 2011. "Employer-to-Employer Flows in the United States: Estimates Using Linked Employer-Employee Data." *Journal of Business and Economic Statistics*, 29(4): 493-505.

Crump, Richard and Aysegul Sahin. 2012. "Skills Mismatch, Construction Workers, and the Labor Market" *Liberty Street Economics*, March 29, 2012. Federal Reserve Bank of New York.

Davis, Steven, John Haltiwanger and Scott Schuh. 1996. *Job Creation and Destruction*. Cambridge, MA: MIT Press.

Fallick, Bruce C. (1996). "A Review of the Recent Empirical Literature on Displaced Workers," *Industrial and Labor Relations Review,* vol. 50, no. 1, pp. 5-16.

Fallick, Bruce, and Charles Fleischman. 2004. "Employer-to-Employer Flows in the U.S. Labor Market: The Complete Picture of Gross Worker Flows." Federal Reserve Board Finance and Economics Discussion Series Working Paper 2004-34.

Fallick, Bruce, John Haltiwanger, and Erika McEntarfer. 2011. "Nonemployment Duration and the Consequences of Job Separations." unpublished working paper (available at: http://www.sole-jole.org/11156.pdf).

Fang, Lei and Pedro Silos, "Are Unemployed Construction Workers Really Doing Better?" *macroblog*. March 30, 2012. Federal Reserve Bank of Atlanta.

Farber, Henry, 2011 "Job Loss in the Great Recession: Historical Perspective from the Displaced Workers Survey, 1984-2010." IZA Discussion Paper No. 5696.

Golan, Amos, Julia Lane and Erika McEntarfer. 2007. "The Dynamics of Worker Reallocation Within and Across Industries." *Economica*, 74(1): 1-20.

Groshen, Erica and Simon Potter. 2003. "Has Structural Change Contributed to a Jobless Recovery," *Current Issues in Economics and Finance*, 9(8).

Hyatt, Henry and Erika McEntarfer. 2012. "Job-to-Job Flows in the Great Recession" *American Economic Review: Papers & Proceedings 2012*, Vol. 102: Iss. 3: 580–583.

Jacobson, Louis, Robert LaLonde and Daniel Sullivan. 1993. "Earnings Losses of Displaced Workers." *American Economic Review*, 83(4): 685-709.

Kambourov, Gueorgui and Iourii Manovskii. 2009. "Occupational Specificity of Human Capital." *International Economic Review*, 50(1): 63-115.

Keith, Kristen and Abigail McWilliams. 1999. "The Returns to Mobility and Job Search by Gender." *Industrial and Labor Relations Review*, 52(3): 460-477.

Lazear, Edward and Jim Spletzer. 2012. "Hiring, Churn and the Business Cycle." *American Economic Review: Papers & Proceedings 2012*, Vol. 102: Iss. 3: 575-579.

Neal, Derek, 1995. "Industry-Specific Human Capital: Evidence from Displaced Workers." *Journal of Labor Economics*, 13(4): 653-677.

Parent, Daniel. "Industry-Specific Capital and the Wage Profile: Evidence from the National Longitudinal Survey of Youth and the Panel Study of Income Dynamics." *Journal of Labor Economics*, 18(2): 306-323.

Poletaev, Maxim and Chris Robinson, 2008. "Human Capital Specificity: Evidence from the Dictionary of Occupational Titles and Displaced Worker Surveys, 1984–2000." *Journal of Labor Economics*, 26 (3): 387-420.

Topel, Robert. 1991. "Specific Capital, Mobility, and Wages: Wages Rise with Job Seniority." *Journal of Political Economy*, 99(1): 145-176.

Topel, Robert and Michael Ward. 1992. "Job Mobility and the Careers of Young Men." *Quarterly Journal of Economics*, 107(2): 439-479.

Appendix: Job-to-Job Flow Definitions

We take employed individuals to be the primary unit of analysis, and allow each employed individual to have one job per quarter, which is that individual's "dominant job." For those with multiple jobs, the dominant job is the employer at which an individual earns the most wages in that quarter. We consider flows into and from dominant jobs, along with associated durations of nonemployment that may exist between different jobs. We also consider the wages associated with a subset of job-to-job flows: those where an individual separates from full-quarter employment and accedes to full-quarter employment. These concepts build on the work of Bjelland et al. (2011) and also Haltiwanger, Fallick, & McEntarfer (2011).

These concepts are defined for each person i. We begin by repeating the definitions of Flow Employment defined in Abowd et al. (2009), where w_{ijt} is the total earnings of individual i at employer j in quarter t.

$$m_{ijt} = \begin{cases} 1, \text{ if } w_{ijt} > 0 \\ 0, \text{ otherwise} \end{cases}$$

We now introduce the concept of a dominant job, which is similar to (but not identical with) the definition of a dominant job employed by Jacobson, Lalonde and Sullivan (1993). We define this measure on a quarterly basis for all individuals i (note that exact ties are extremely rare).

$$d_{ijt} = \begin{cases} 1, \text{ if } w_{ijt} > w_{imt} \ \forall j \neq m \\ 0, \text{ otherwise} \end{cases}$$

Note that the following flows are set to zero. If an individual is continuously employed with a dominant employer in an employer, with that employer dominant in the previous and subsequent quarter, the employer is also set to be dominant in the referenced (middle) quarter.

Full-quarter employment is defined, following Abowd et al. (2009) as

$$f_{ijt} = \begin{cases} 1, \text{ if } m_{ijt-1} = 1 \text{ and } m_{ijt} = 1 \text{ and } m_{ijt+1} = 1 \\ 0, \text{ otherwise} \end{cases}$$

We now define a series of relationships between dominant employers: origin employer j, destination employer k, where the origin employer is a dominant employer in quarter t and the destination employer is a dominant employer in either the subsequent quarter $t+1$, or (in the case of an intervening spell of nonemployment) another future quarter. Transitions that are of primary interest are those that are conventionally considered as employment transitions: where employment ends with a separation, and begins with an accession. All such flows are defined where $j \neq k$.

The first two job-to-job flows includes any case in which the accession and separation occur within the same quarter. These includes cases in which there is no spell of nonemployment, or when that spell is rather short (less than 13 weeks), or even cases in which there is a small amount of overlap of the old job and new job. Where the separation from the origin employer occurs in quarter t, we define

$$dd_{ijkt0_A} = \begin{cases} 1, \text{if } d_{ijt} = 1 \text{ and } m_{ijt+1} = 0 \text{ and } m_{ikt-1} = 0 \text{ and } m_{ikt} = 1 \text{ and } d_{ikt+1} = 1 \\ 0, \text{otherwise} \end{cases}$$

and where the separation from the origin employer occurs in quarter $t+1$, we define

$$dd_{ijkt0_B} = \begin{cases} 1, \text{if } d_{ijt} = 1 \text{ and } m_{ijt+1} = 1 \text{ and } m_{ijt+2} = 0 \text{ and } m_{ikt} = 0 \text{ and } d_{ikt+1} = 1 \\ 0, \text{otherwise} \end{cases}$$

For cases in which the separation and subsequent accession occur in adjacent quarters, we define

$$dd_{ijkt1} = \begin{cases} 1, \text{if } d_{ijt} = 1 \text{ and } m_{ijt+1} = 0 \text{ and } m_{ikt} = 0 \text{ and } d_{ikt+1} = 1 \\ 0, \text{otherwise} \end{cases}$$

which would not include any spell of nonemployment for cases in which the separation and accession occur immediately before and after, respectively, the date on which a quarter starts, but may frequently imply some small duration of nonemployment.

For job-to-job flows with a nonemployment spell, for any $p \geq 2$

$$dd_{ijktp} = \begin{cases} 1, \text{if } d_{ijt} = 1 \text{ and } w_{i \cdot t+1} = \cdots = w_{i \cdot t+p-1} = 0 \text{ and } d_{ikt+p} = 1 \\ 0, \text{otherwise} \end{cases}$$

where $w_{i \cdot t}$ is the total earnings of individual i in quarter t.

Of course, not all transitions from one dominant job to another involves a separation from the origin dominant employer and an accession to a dominant employer. Therefore, for completeness, we can define dominant job-to dominant job transitions where this is not the case. For all such spells, there is no intervening spell of full-quarter nonemployment, so we continue to subscript these dominant job-to-dominant job flows as dd_{ijkt0_K}, where K indexes the flow type. When there is no coincidental accession (and so a continuing job becomes a main job), we define

$$dd_{ijkt0_C} = \begin{cases} 1, \text{if } d_{ijt} = 1 \text{ and } m_{ijt+1} = 0 \text{ and } m_{ikt-1} = 1 \text{ and } m_{ikt} = 1 \text{ and } d_{ikt+1} = 1 \\ 0, \text{otherwise} \end{cases}$$

and

$$dd_{ijkt0_D} = \begin{cases} 1, \text{if } d_{ijt} = 1 \text{ and } m_{ijt+1} = 1 \text{ and } m_{ijt+2} = 0 \text{ and } m_{ikt} = 1 \text{ and } d_{ikt+1} = 1 \\ 0, \text{otherwise} \end{cases}$$

When there is an accession but no coincidental separation, we define

$$dd_{ijkt0_E} = \begin{cases} 1, \text{if } d_{ijt} = 1 \text{ and } m_{ijt+1} = 1 \text{ and } m_{ikt-1} = 0 \text{ and } m_{ikt} = 1 \text{ and } d_{ikt+1} = 1 \\ 0, \text{otherwise} \end{cases}$$

and

$$dd_{ijkt0_F} = \begin{cases} 1, \text{if } d_{ijt} = 1 \text{ and } m_{ijt+1} = 1 \text{ and } m_{ijt+2} = 1 \text{ and } m_{ikt} = 0 \text{ and } d_{ikt+1} = 1 \\ 0, \text{otherwise} \end{cases}$$

For transitions where there is no separation from the origin job, we define dominant job-to-dominant job flows as follows.

$$dd_{ijkt0_G} = \begin{cases} 1, \text{if } d_{ijt} = 1 \text{ and } m_{ijt+1} = m_{ijt+2} = m_{ikt-1} = m_{ikt} = 1 \text{ and } d_{ikt+1} = 1 \\ 0, \text{otherwise} \end{cases}$$

Analogous full-quarter measures for transitions between dominant employers are as follows

$$ff_{ijkt0_A}^d = \begin{cases} 1, \text{if } dd_{ijkt0_A} = 1 \text{ and } f_{ijt-1} = 1 \text{ and } f_{ikt+1} = 1 \\ 0, \text{otherwise} \end{cases}$$

$$ff_{ijkt0_B}^d = \begin{cases} 1, \text{if } dd_{ijkt0_B} = 1 \text{ and } f_{ijt} = 1 \text{ and } f_{ikt+2} = 1 \\ 0, \text{otherwise} \end{cases}$$

$$ff_{ijkt1}^d = \begin{cases} 1, \text{if } dd_{ijkt1} = 1 \text{ and } f_{ijt-1} = 1 \text{ and } f_{ikt+2} = 1 \\ 0, \text{otherwise} \end{cases}$$

And similarly for any $p \geq 2$

$$ff_{ijktp}^d = \begin{cases} 1, \text{if } dd_{ijktp} = 1 \text{ and } f_{ijt-1} = 1 \text{ and } f_{ikt+p+1} = 1 \\ 0, \text{otherwise} \end{cases}$$

Exiting earnings is defined as full quarter earnings for the subsets of individuals for whom the respective conditions hold. Wages at separation are defined at wages are, by job flow type,

$$WSff_{ijkt0_A}^d = \begin{cases} w_{ijt-1}, \text{if } ff_{ijkt0_A}^d = 1 \\ \text{undefined, otherwise} \end{cases}$$

$$WSff_{ijkt0_B}^d = \begin{cases} w_{ijt}, \text{if } ff_{ijkt0_B}^d = 1 \\ \text{undefined, otherwise} \end{cases}$$

And for all $p > 0$

$$WSff_{ijktp}^d = \begin{cases} w_{ijt-1}, \text{if } ff_{ijktp}^d = 1 \\ \text{undefined, otherwise} \end{cases}$$

And accessions are as follows:

$$WAff_{ijkt0_A}^d = \begin{cases} w_{ikt+1}, \text{if } ff_{ijkt0_A}^d = 1 \\ \text{undefined, otherwise} \end{cases}$$

$$WAff_{ijkt0_B}^d = \begin{cases} w_{ikt+2}, \text{if } ff_{ijkt0_B}^d = 1 \\ \text{undefined, otherwise} \end{cases}$$

And similarly for $p > 0$

$$WAff_{ijktp}^d = \begin{cases} w_{ikt+p+1}, \text{if } ff_{ijktp}^d = 1 \\ \text{undefined, otherwise} \end{cases}$$

Note that wages for origin and destination job-to-job flow types 0_C, 0_D, 0_E, 0_F and 0_G are defined analogously.

Figure 1: Total Dominant Job Separations, by Nonemployment: 1998:2-2010:2 (In Thousands)

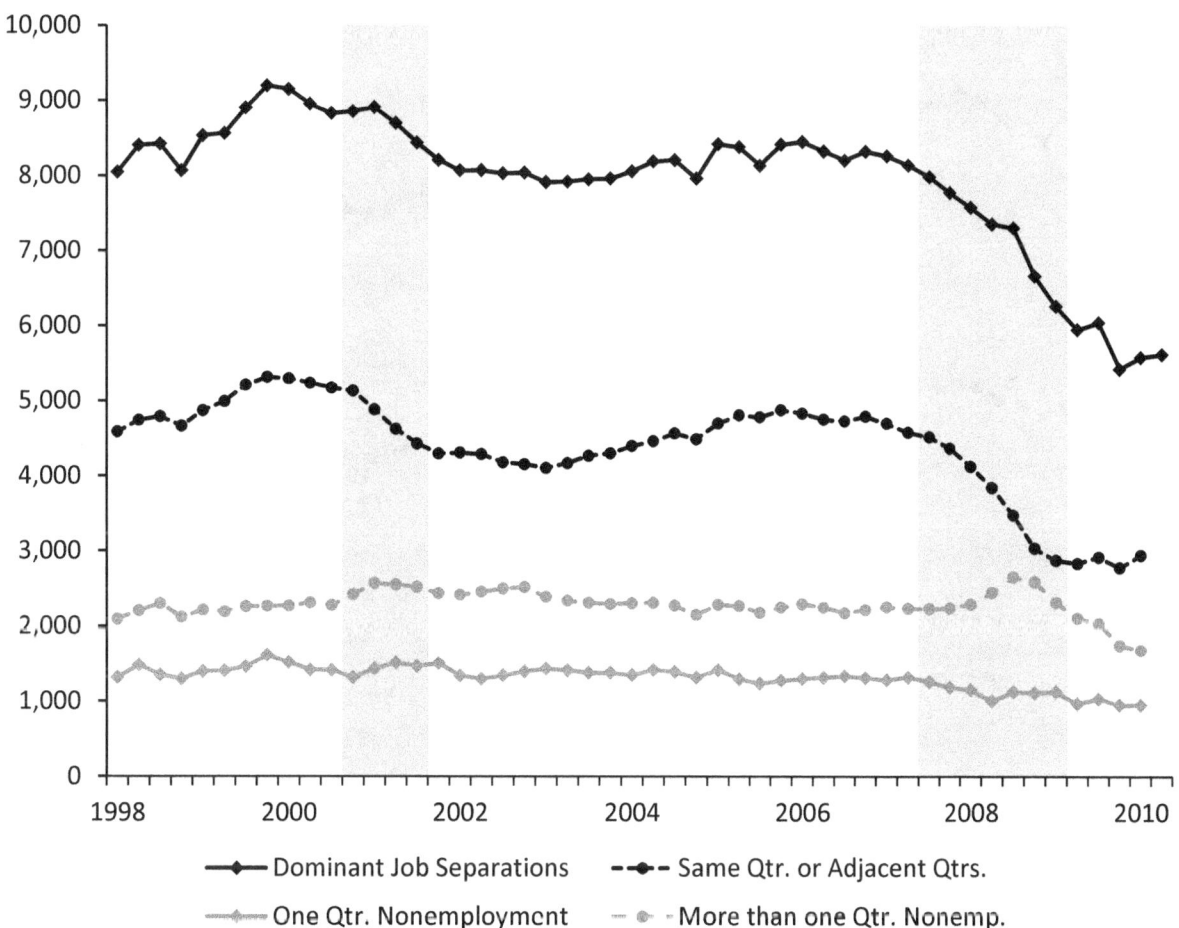

Notes: Shaded areas denote NBER recession quarters. Calculated from LEHD 40-state employment histories for worker who worked in any of nine states, see text for details. The data in this figure also appears in Figure 1 of Hyatt and McEntarfer (2011).

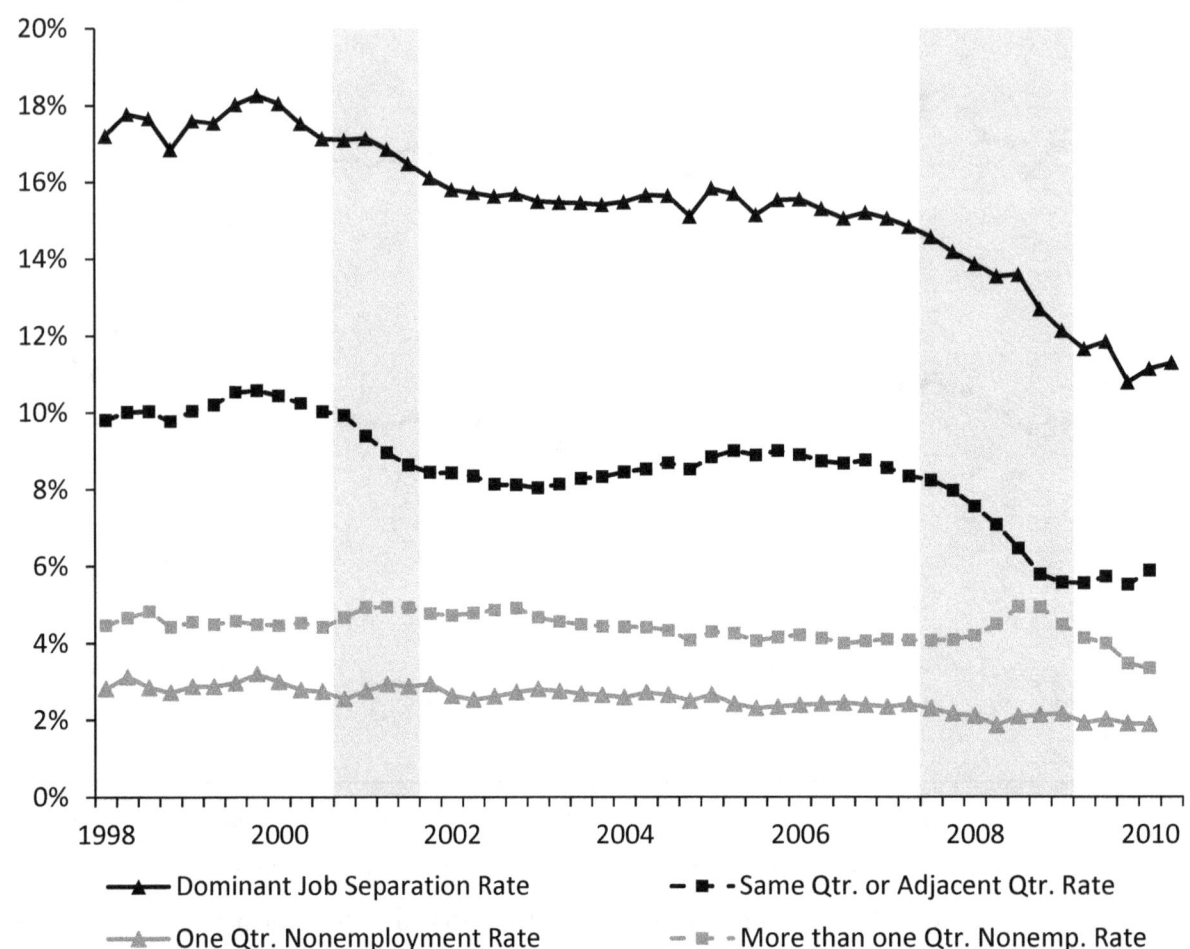

Figure 2: Dominant Job Separation Rate, by Nonemployment 1998:2-2010:2

Legend:
—▲— Dominant Job Separation Rate   – ■ – Same Qtr. or Adjacent Qtr. Rate
—▲— One Qtr. Nonemployment Rate   – ■ – More than one Qtr. Nonemp. Rate

Notes: Shaded areas denote NBER recession quarters. Calculated from LEHD 40-state employment histories for worker who worked in any of nine states, see text for details.

Figure 3: Job-to-Job Flow Rates by Age: 1998:2-2010:2 (Within- and Adjacent Quarters Only)

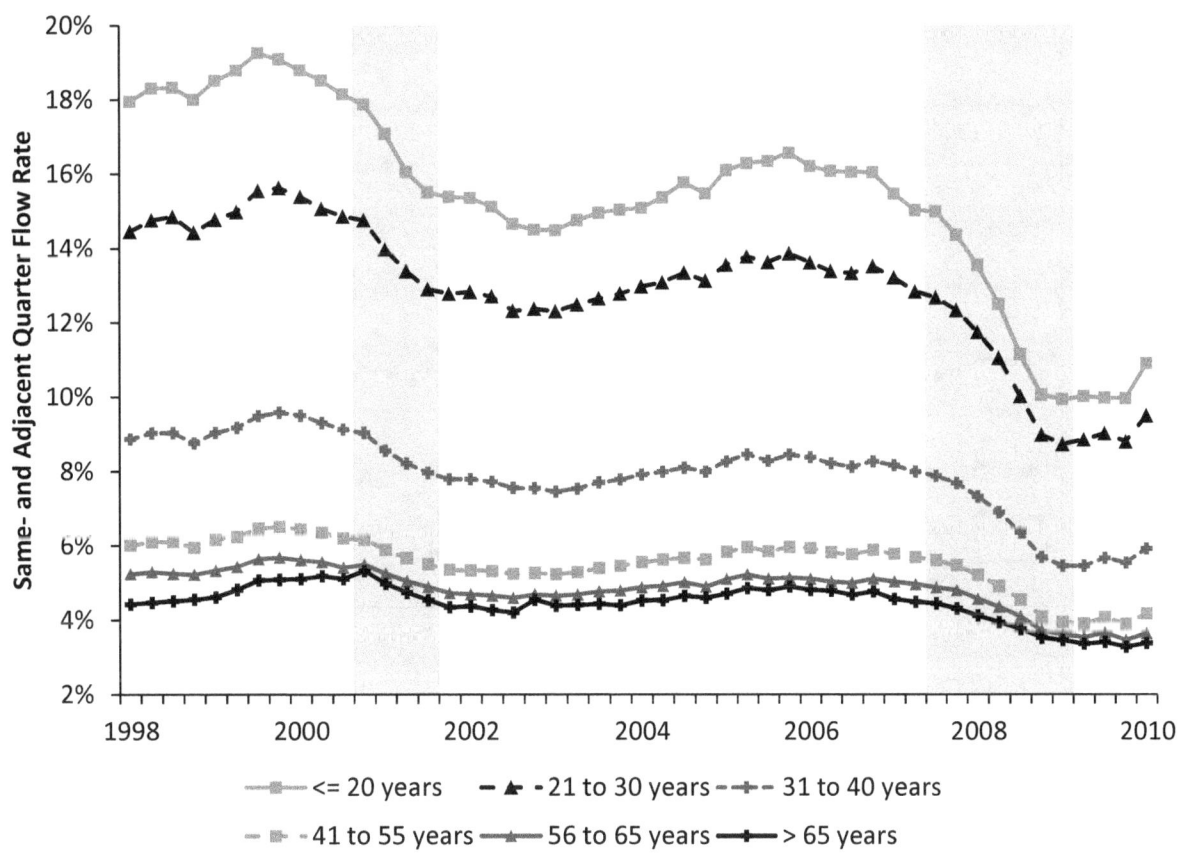

Notes: Shaded areas denote NBER recession quarters. Calculated from LEHD 40-state employment histories for worker who worked in any of nine states, see text for details.

Figure 4: Median Change in Real Earnings from Job Change, by Age (No Nonemployment)

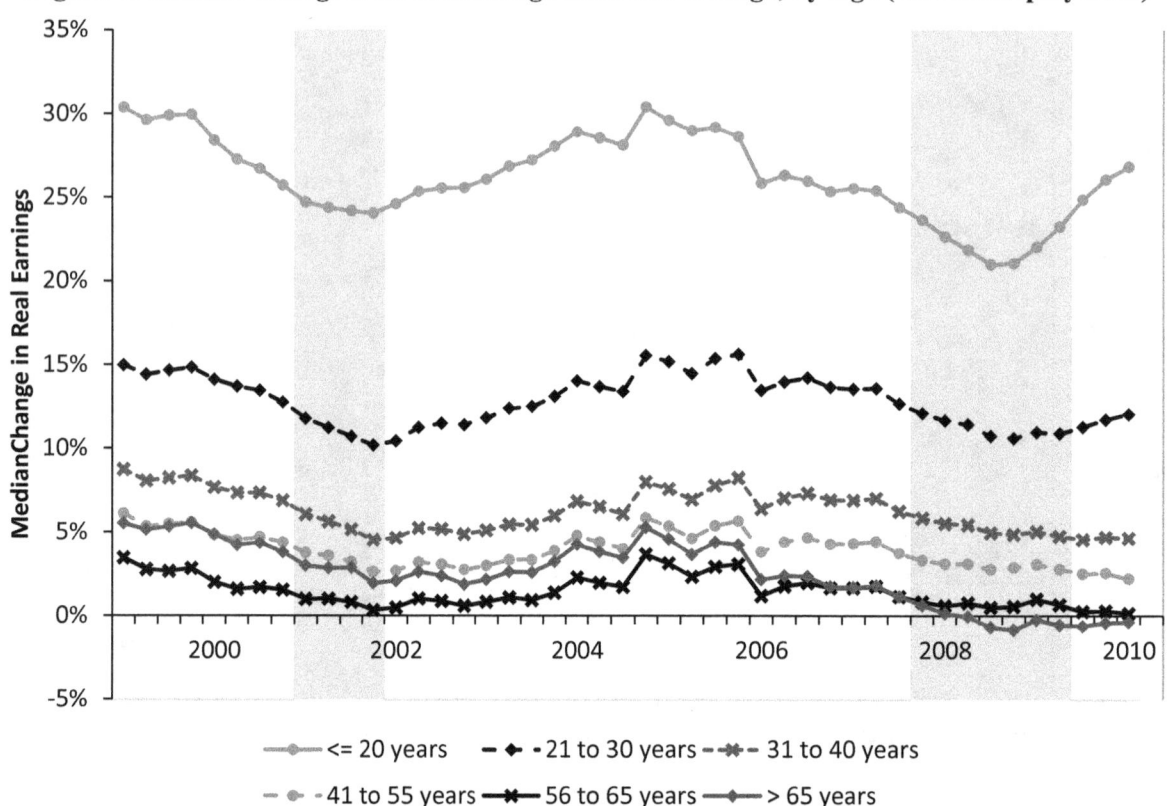

Notes: Earnings changes are for jobs that survive the quarter only (i.e. a full-quarter of earnings must be observed in both origin and destination job). Shaded areas denote NBER recession quarters. . Calculated from LEHD 40-state employment histories for worker who worked in any of nine states, see text for details.

Figure 5: Median Change in Real Earnings from Job Change, by Nonemployment Duration

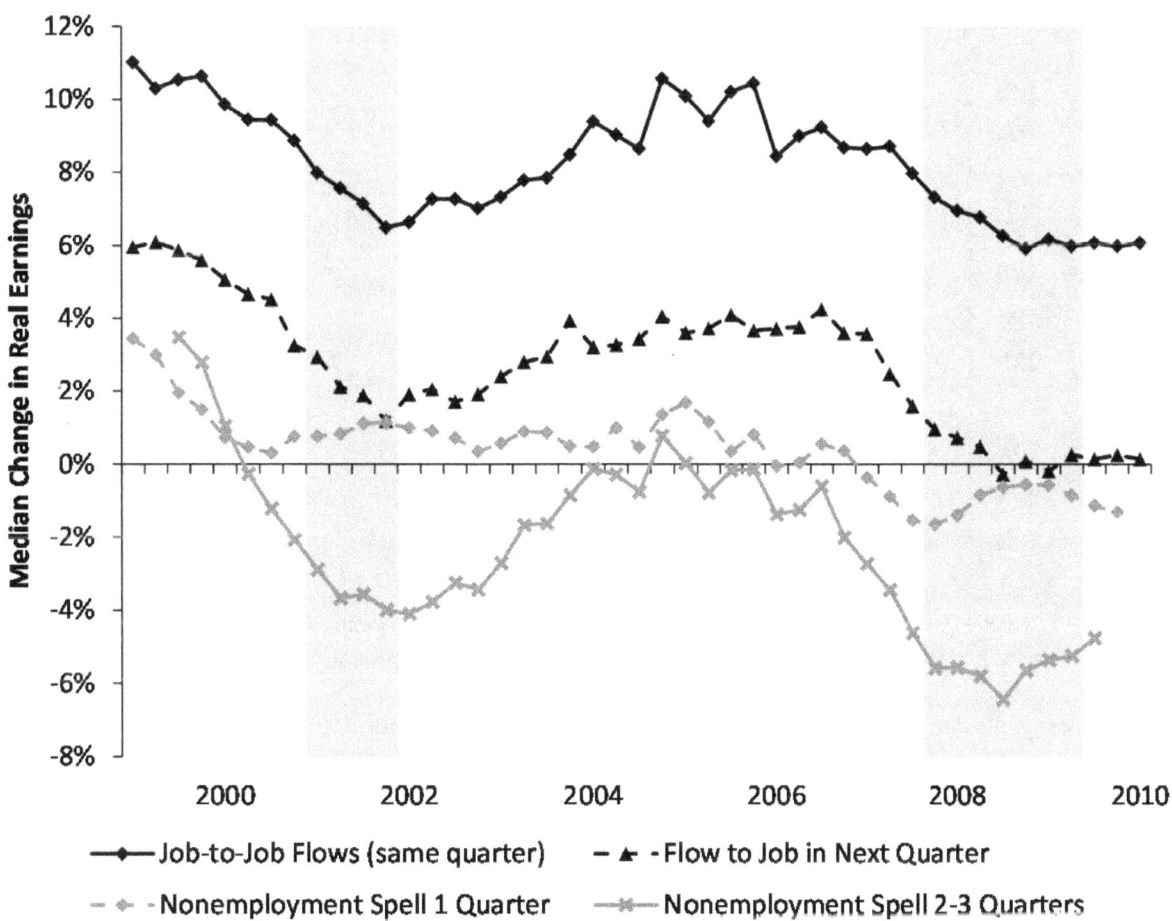

Notes: Earnings changes are for jobs that survive the quarter only (i.e. a full-quarter of earnings must be observed in both origin and destination job). Shaded areas denote NBER recession quarters. Calculated from LEHD microdata, national employment histories for workers in nine states. The data in this figure also appears in Figure 2 of Hyatt and McEntarfer (2011).

Figure 6: Mass Layoff Events in 2000-2001 and 2007-2008,
Real total quarterly earnings changes, prime age men, relative to pre-separation earnings

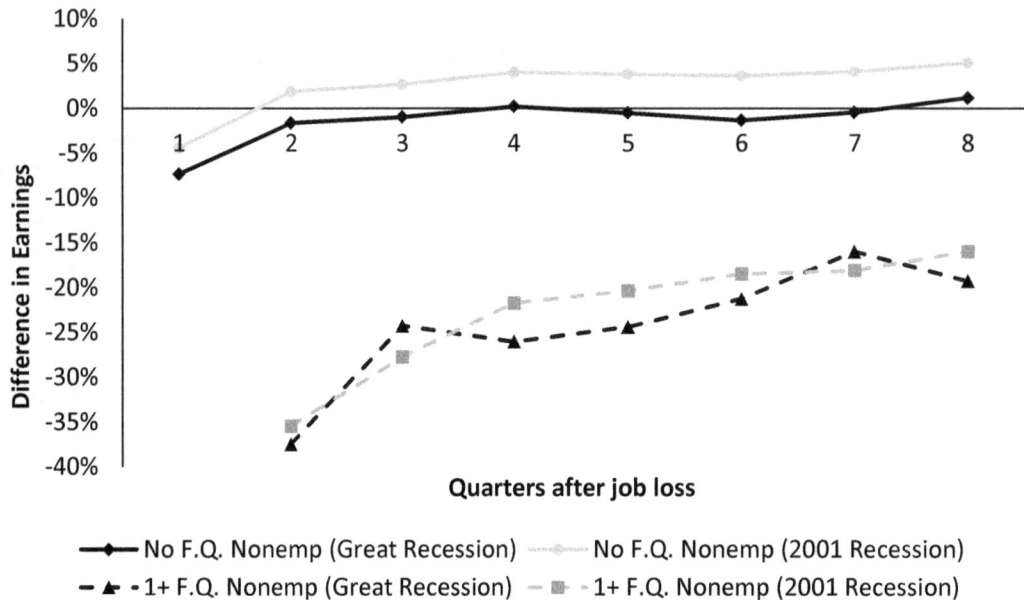

Notes: Calculated from LEHD microdata, national employment histories for workers in nine states.

Figure 7: Mass Layoff Events in 2000-2001 and 2007-2008.
Share with zero earnings, Prime age men.

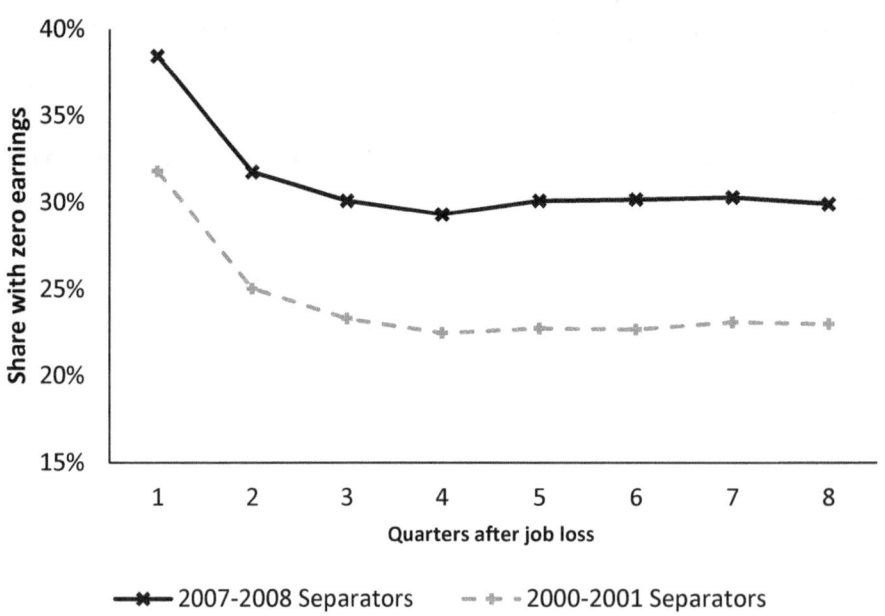

Notes: Calculated from LEHD microdata, national employment histories for workers in nine states.

**Figure 8: Mass Layoff Events in 2007-2008, Selected Industries.
Real total quarterly earnings changes, relative to pre-separation earnings**

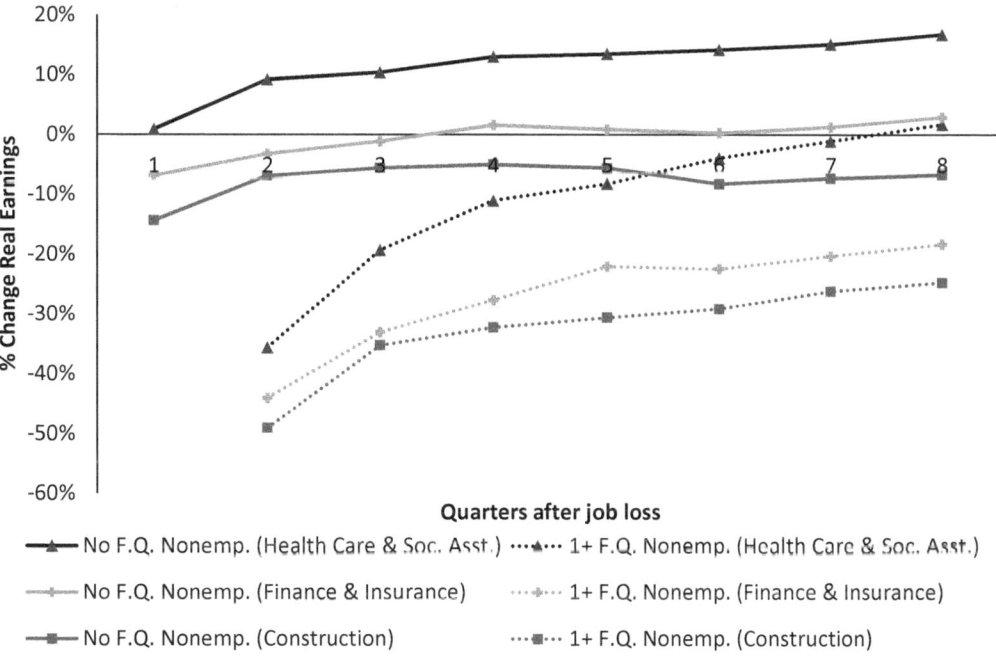

- No F.Q. Nonemp. (Health Care & Soc. Asst.)
- 1+ F.Q. Nonemp. (Health Care & Soc. Asst.)
- No F.Q. Nonemp. (Finance & Insurance)
- 1+ F.Q. Nonemp. (Finance & Insurance)
- No F.Q. Nonemp. (Construction)
- 1+ F.Q. Nonemp. (Construction)

**Figure 9: Mass Layoff Events in 2007-2008, Selected Industries.
Share with zero earnings, prime age men.**

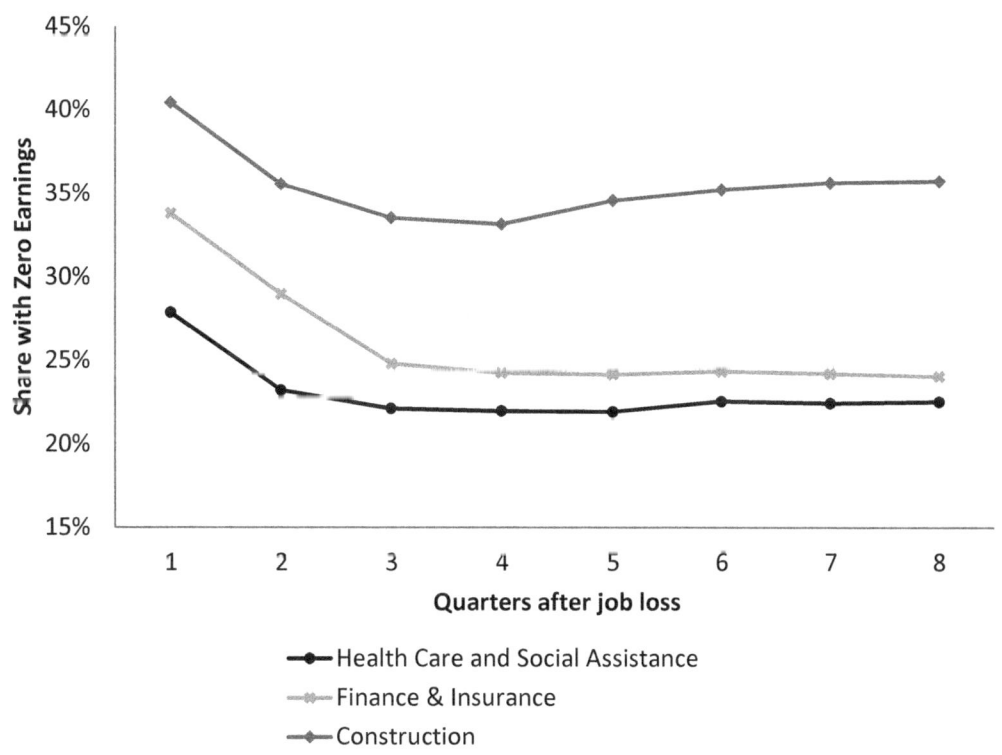

- Health Care and Social Assistance
- Finance & Insurance
- Construction

Table 1: Origin-destination matrix of NAICS Supersector Transitions, 1999-2009

Origin Supersector	Nat'l Resources and Mining	Trade, Trans. and Utilities	Construction	Manufacturing	Information	Financial Activities	Prof. and bus. Services	Educ. and Health Care	Leisure and Hospitality	Other Services	Public Administration*	N (in 1000's)
					Destination Supersector							
Nat'l Resources and Mining	54.5	9.7	6.7	7.4	0.3	1.2	10.1	2.5	5.4	1.4	0.7	2,198
Trade, Trans. and Utilities	1.0	43.8	4.2	6.3	1.9	4.4	15.0	7.8	11.0	3.1	1.6	20,480
Construction	1.9	9.4	55.6	5.5	0.8	2.3	13.5	2.7	5.3	2.0	1.0	7,099
Manufacturing	2.2	18.5	7.2	32.5	1.6	2.3	20.8	4.8	6.7	2.4	1.2	6,875
Information	0.3	13.9	2.3	3.8	32.5	5.4	24.3	6.1	8.2	1.9	1.3	2,445
Financial Activities	0.5	12.5	3.5	2.8	2.5	41.6	17.8	8.0	7.0	2.2	1.5	4,986
Prof. and Business Services	1.1	15.3	5.3	12.1	3.5	5.8	37.1	8.5	7.5	2.2	1.5	20,522
Education and Health Care	0.4	9.0	1.5	2.3	1.1	3.0	12.8	56.8	6.9	2.9	3.2	12,413
Leisure and Hospitality	0.8	17.9	3.1	3.7	1.5	3.4	12.8	8.2	44.7	2.8	1.3	15,212
Other Services	1.0	19.3	5.3	5.2	1.5	3.9	14.8	12.8	11.8	22.0	2.2	3,002
Public Administration*	0.8	13.2	3.7	3.2	1.4	3.5	13.8	20.6	8.0	4.7	27.1	1,595

Notes: Calculated from LEHD microdata, national employment histories for workers in nine states. Only flows with both an origin and a destination industry are included.

* Public Aministration does not include federal workers due to data availability.

Table 2: Median percent change in Earnings, 1999-2009

Origin Supersector	Destination Supersector										
	Nat'l Resources and Mining	Trade, Trans. and Utilities	Construction	Manufacturing	Information	Financial Activities	Prof. and bus. Services	Educ. and Health Care	Leisure and Hospitality	Other Services	Public Administration*
Nat'l Resources and Mining	6	2	12	9	4	5	3	-3	-15	-6	-3
Trade, Trans. and Utilities	15	7	15	15	18	17	11	17	2	6	19
Construction	5	2	7	7	9	3	2	-4	-22	-2	0
Manufacturing	6	1	7	6	5	2	0	-10	-23	-6	-4
Information	4	5	4	9	6	5	5	1	-1	1	6
Financial Activities	7	4	8	12	10	5	5	3	-8	0	8
Prof. and Business Services	14	11	14	16	12	13	7	11	0	7	14
Education and Health Care	19	12	18	30	22	16	10	8	0	6	16
Leisure and Hospitality	30	25	37	41	32	31	23	31	7	18	37
Other Services	21	13	18	20	19	16	13	16	6	4	13
Public Administration*	18	5	13	20	15	10	10	3	-7	2	3

Notes: Calculated from LEHD microdata, national employment histories for workers in nine states. Only flows with an origin and destination are included.
* Public Aministration does not include federal workers due to data availability.

Table 3: Nonemployment characteristics of dominant job changes, 1999-2009

Origin Supersector	Within-quarter EE flow	Adjacent-quarter EE flow	Flow with 1 quarter nonemp	Flow with 2-3 Quarters Nonemp	Flow with 4+ quarters nonemp	Separation without observed accession	Secondary job becomes main	New main job, former main job becomes secondary
Nat'l Resources and Mining	17.6	28.5	19.6	13.8	10.7	6.6	1.5	1.7
Trade, Trans. and Utilities	25.2	26.5	16.0	11.0	11.3	6.2	1.3	2.5
Construction	21.8	30.5	17.0	10.3	10.5	6.4	1.8	1.6
Manufacturing	22.9	24.6	17.4	12.2	11.1	8.2	1.9	1.7
Information	24.2	26.6	16.8	11.0	10.7	5.0	2.1	3.7
Financial Activities	28.1	25.0	15.1	10.7	10.7	6.9	1.6	2.0
Prof. and Business Services	25.9	28.9	15.1	10.8	10.8	5.6	1.3	1.7
Education and Health Care	22.0	21.6	19.9	11.8	10.7	7.5	2.5	4.0
Leisure and Hospitality	22.5	28.9	15.1	12.0	11.5	5.4	1.4	3.2
Other Services	18.9	24.7	16.5	12.2	13.1	9.3	2.0	3.4
Public Administration*	19.0	16.2	22.2	15.8	11.0	10.1	2.8	2.9

Notes: Calculated from LEHD microdata, national employment histories for workers in nine states.

*: Public Administration does not include federal workers due to data availability.

Table 4: Wage changes, by origin supersector and nonemployment, 1999-2009

Origin Supersector	Within-quarter EE flow	Adjacent-quarter EE flow	Flow with 1 quarter nonemp	Flow with 2-3 Quarters Nonemp	Flow with 4+ quarters nonemp	Separation without observed accession	Secondary job becomes main	New main job, former main job becomes secondary
Nat'l Resources and Mining	6.0	1.0	0.0	-2.0	-4.0	-	-32.0	18.0
Trade, Trans. and Utilities	10.0	3.0	0.0	-2.0	-2.0	-	-22.0	14.0
Construction	6.0	0.0	-1.0	-4.0	-10.0	-	-33.0	1.0
Manufacturing	3.0	-4.0	-2.0	-12.0	-23.0	-	-32.0	10.0
Information	6.0	0.0	-1.0	-7.0	-19.0	-	-38.0	8.0
Financial Activities	5.0	0.0	-1.0	-10.0	-18.0	-	-33.0	10.0
Prof. and Business Services	11.0	4.0	0.0	-3.0	-6.0	-	-29.0	10.0
Education and Health Care	10.0	5.0	1.0	0.0	3.0	-	-13.0	6.0
Leisure and Hospitality	18.0	11.0	3.0	11.0	19.0	-	-12.0	16.0
Other Services	12.0	6.0	0.0	0.0	2.0	-	-27.0	29.0
Public Administration*	5.0	-1.0	2.0	0.0	-12.0	-	-25.0	13.0

Notes: Calculated from LEHD microdata, national employment histories for workers in nine states. Only flows with three or fewer quarters of nonemployment are included.

*: Public Administration does not include federal workers due to data availability.

Table 5: Percent of Separations from Employment Without Nonemployment, 1999-2009

Origin Supersector	1999	2000	2001	2002	2003	2004	2005	2006	2007	2008	2009
Nat'l Resources and Mining	19.6	19.8	19.1	19.1	18.9	20.1	22.5	22.9	22.8	21.9	20.2
Trade, Trans. and Utilities	30.1	30.5	28.2	27.4	27.4	28.5	30.8	30.7	30.3	28.6	24.8
Construction	26.2	26.4	24.9	24.1	23.3	25.2	26.9	27.5	26.8	24.1	19.4
Manufacturing	28.6	29.3	25.6	24.1	23.6	26.3	28.5	29.1	28.3	25.1	18.5
Information	30.9	32.9	27.9	26.8	26.6	29.4	31.4	32.7	32.1	30.3	27.2
Financial Activities	32.7	34.4	31.3	30.2	29.6	31.0	33.7	33.5	32.9	30.7	26.5
Prof. and Business Services	30.0	30.4	27.4	26.4	26.5	28.6	30.4	31.3	31.1	28.8	24.7
Education and Health Care	28.9	30.3	28.4	27.6	25.5	27.3	29.2	30.4	29.8	29.5	25.9
Leisure and Hospitality	27.5	27.5	25.6	25.7	25.5	26.7	28.3	28.6	28.4	27.0	25.2
Other Services	24.9	25.1	22.8	22.7	22.7	24.0	25.5	26.1	26.3	24.3	21.4
Public Administration*	23.4	26.7	25.1	21.9	22.9	24.5	27.8	26.9	27.2	24.6	20.8

Notes: Calculated from LEHD microdata, national employment histories for workers in nine states.

* Public Aministration does not include federal workers due to data availability.

Table 6: Percent of Separations Within-Industry (Without Nonemployment), 1999-2009

Origin Supersector	1999	2000	2001	2002	2003	2004	2005	2006	2007	2008	2009
Nat'l Resources and Mining	53.8	51.9	52.9	54.3	54.2	52.8	53.1	53.5	54.8	58.0	60.5
Trade, Trans. and Utilities	43.4	42.7	43.2	44.0	44.6	44.1	44.0	43.8	43.8	43.8	44.7
Construction	55.9	55.7	56.7	56.6	57.1	56.4	56.3	54.6	54.1	53.8	53.5
Manufacturing	35.5	35.5	31.1	31.8	31.4	32.7	32.5	32.1	30.7	30.7	27.8
Information	31.2	31.3	28.7	32.4	32.0	33.2	31.7	33.6	33.6	35.0	38.0
Financial Activities	39.3	37.9	40.3	42.1	43.5	43.4	43.9	42.7	41.5	40.3	43.9
Prof. and Business Services	36.2	35.9	35.3	36.4	36.6	37.2	37.6	37.6	38.0	38.0	39.8
Education and Health Care	53.6	53.6	56.4	56.8	56.6	56.5	56.6	56.7	57.6	59.6	61.7
Leisure and Hospitality	43.0	42.3	43.7	44.1	44.6	44.5	44.1	44.7	45.6	47.1	49.0
Other Services	20.1	19.4	21.5	22.9	23.4	22.0	21.5	21.5	22.4	23.6	25.9
Public Administration*	24.5	29.9	29.9	26.1	25.6	26.4	25.6	27.3	27.4	28.5	25.8

Notes: Calculated from LEHD microdata, national employment histories for workers in nine states. Only flows in which the separation and accession occur in the same quarter or in which the quarter of accession immediately follows the quarter of separation are included.

* Public Aministration does not include federal workers due to data availability.

Table 7: Median percent change in wages for separators, by supersector

Origin Supersector	1999	2000	2001	2002	2003	2004	2005	2006	2007	2008	2009
Nat'l Resources and Mining	2	0	2	0	1	1	3	3	-1	-1	-2
Trade, Trans. and Utilities	9	6	3	3	4	6	6	6	4	1	2
Construction	5	3	1	0	1	3	3	2	-1	-3	-3
Manufacturing	2	-1	-3	-3	-2	-1	-1	-1	-2	-4	-2
Information	8	4	-2	-2	1	1	2	3	1	0	-2
Financial Activities	5	3	1	0	0	2	2	2	0	-1	-1
Prof. and Business Services	11	8	3	4	5	7	8	7	5	3	2
Education and Health Care	6	6	5	4	3	4	5	5	3	4	1
Leisure and Hospitality	16	13	11	12	13	14	14	14	11	7	8
Other Services	9	6	4	4	5	5	6	6	4	2	2
Public Administration*	3	1	3	2	2	1	3	2	1	1	-1

Notes: Calculated from LEHD microdata, national employment histories for workers in nine states. Only flows which involve
* Public Aministration does not include federal workers due to data availability.

Table 8: Nonemployment for Separations from Selected Industries

Flow Type, by NAICS Sector	Frequency of Destinations			Wage Change (Median)		
	2001-03	2004-06	2007-09	2001-03	2004-06	2007-09
Construction	**100.0**	**100.0**	**100.0**	**0.8**	**2.4**	**-2.0**
No Full-Quarter Non-employment	52.8	56.5	51.5	2.6	4.9	0.2
Sep. & Access. in same Qtr.	21.8	23.8	20.8	4.9	7.1	3.8
Access. in Qtr. after Sep.	31.1	32.7	30.7	0.0	2.0	-3.2
One Full Qtr. of Non-emp.	18.4	17.0	17.2	0.1	-0.1	-3.0
Two Qtrs. of Non-emp.	7.0	6.5	7.1	-1.9	-2.5	-10.5
Three Qtrs. of Non-emp.	4.0	3.8	4.2	-4.9	-3.6	-15.2
Four or more Qtrs. of Non-emp.	17.7	16.3	20.1	-	-	-
Manufacturing	**100.0**	**100.0**	**100.0**	**-3.0**	**-1.2**	**-3.0**
No Full-Quarter Non-employment	47.1	51.4	43.7	-1.3	1.4	-1.1
Sep. & Access. in same Qtr.	21.9	25.2	21.2	1.7	4.0	2.3
Access. in Qtr. after Sep.	25.2	26.2	22.4	-6.4	-3.1	-6.5
One Full Qtr. of Non-emp.	18.7	17.6	17.1	-0.7	-1.4	-2.0
Two Qtrs. of Non-emp.	8.1	7.3	7.9	-11.3	-10.8	-11.7
Three Qtrs. of Non-emp.	4.9	5.2	7.0	-18.6	-17.2	-15.5
Four or more Qtrs. of Non-emp.	21.2	18.4	24.3	-	-	-
Finance & Insurance	**100.0**	**100.0**	**100.0**	**0.2**	**1.7**	**-0.9**
No Full-Quarter Non-employment	55.3	57.7	53.5	2.3	4.0	0.8
Sep. & Access. in same Qtr.	30.0	32.1	29.2	4.3	5.9	3.0
Access. in Qtr. after Sep.	25.3	25.6	24.3	-1.6	0.2	-2.4
One Full Qtr. of Non-emp.	16.2	15.6	14.9	0.0	0.0	-1.8
Two Qtrs. of Non-emp.	6.6	6.2	6.6	-10.6	-8.6	-18.6
Three Qtrs. of Non-emp.	4.3	4.1	4.7	-16.7	-14.2	-23.4
Four or more Qtrs. of Non-emp.	17.6	16.4	20.4	-	-	-
Health Care & Social Assistance	**100.0**	**100.0**	**100.0**	**3.2**	**3.5**	**2.3**
No Full-Quarter Non-employment	52.0	54.0	51.6	5.3	5.8	4.5
Sep. & Access. in same Qtr.	26.6	28.1	27.4	7.2	7.9	6.9
Access. in Qtr. after Sep.	25.4	25.9	24.2	2.0	2.0	0.4
One Full Qtr. of Non-emp.	18.6	18.3	16.9	1.2	0.6	-0.2
Two Qtrs. of Non-emp.	6.8	6.3	6.5	-2.4	-2.2	-3.0
Three Qtrs. of Non-emp.	4.1	4.0	4.3	-2.6	-0.5	-3.4
Four or more Qtrs. of Non-emp.	18.6	17.5	20.7	-	-	-

Notes: Calculated from the set of all job-to-job flows that involve a separation and an accession, in which the separation industry is in the Construction, Manufacturing, Finance & Insurance, or Health Care & Social Assistance NAICS sector. Associated median wage changes are available for the subset of job-to-job flows in which both the separation is from and accession is to full-quarter employment, see text for details. Wage changes are calculated for full-quarter earnings of separation job S and accession job A according to (A-S)/((A+S)/2). Earnings changes for four or more quarters of non-employment are omitted because this category includes non-employment durations of different lengths due to right-censoring in 2010.

Table 9a: Job-to-Job Flows Originating in Construction

Destination Industry	Frequency of Destinations			Wage Change (Median)		
	2001-03	2004-06	2007-09	2001-03	2004-06	2007-09
Any Destination Industry	**100.0**	**100.0**	**100.0**	**2.6**	**4.9**	**0.2**
Agric., Forestry, Fishing & Hunting	1.4	1.5	1.9	-6.3	-4.4	-9.3
Mining, Quarrying and Gas Extraction	0.5	0.6	0.8	17.2	26.0	20.7
Utilities	0.3	0.3	0.3	11.0	13.2	11.1
Construction	**54.0**	**52.0**	**51.0**	**4.9**	**7.0**	**4.0**
Manufacturing	5.2	5.4	4.9	7.1	10.2	5.9
Wholesale Trade	2.3	2.5	2.4	4.8	7.4	4.0
Retail Trade	5.5	5.4	5.2	-2.8	-0.1	-11.0
Transportation & Warehousing	1.8	1.9	1.8	4.5	6.4	0.2
Information	0.7	0.6	0.6	4.8	10.8	7.2
Finance & Insurance	0.8	0.8	0.8	-0.4	2.0	-2.9
Real Estate and Rental and Leasing	1.3	1.4	1.3	2.8	6.2	-0.1
Prof., Sci. & Tech. Services	2.7	2.9	3.2	4.7	7.9	4.6
Mgmt. of Companies & Enterprises	0.5	0.4	0.4	5.5	8.1	5.3
Admin., Suppt. & Waste Mgmt.	11.7	12.7	11.5	-2.0	0.1	-5.3
Educational Sercvices	0.9	0.8	1.0	-7.5	-4.0	-8.5
Health Care & Soc. Assistance	1.4	1.5	2.0	0.9	2.9	-1.4
Arts, Entertainment and Recreation	0.9	0.9	1.0	-8.4	-5.9	-12.5
Accommodation & Food Services	5.1	5.6	6.8	-20.4	-16.9	-24.6
Other Services (Excl. Publ. Admin.)	2.1	2.2	2.5	-0.8	1.1	-2.7
Public Administration*	0.9	0.8	0.9	1.1	1.8	0.9
Job-to-Job Flows (thousands)	3868.1	4441.1	3662.6	990.6	1225.5	1038.2

Notes: Calculated from the set of all job-to-job flows that involve a separation and an accession which are within-quarter or in adjacent quarters, in which the origin industry is in the Construction NAICS sector. Construction is in bold for emphasis. Associated median wage changes are available for the subset of job-to-job flows in which both the separation is from and accession is to full-quarter employment, see text for details. Wage changes are calculated for full-quarter earnings of separation job S and accession job A according to (A-S)/((A+S)/2).

*: Public Administration does not include federal workers due to data availability.

Table 9b: Job-to-Job Flows Originating in Manufacturing

Destination Industry	Frequency of Destinations			Wage Change (Median)		
	2001-03	2004-06	2007-09	2001-03	2004-06	2007-09
Any Destination Industry	**100.0**	**100.0**	**100.0**	**-1.3**	**1.4**	**-1.1**
Agric., Forestry, Fishing & Hunting	2.2	2.1	2.5	-2.2	-1.5	-3.7
Mining, Quarrying and Gas Extraction	0.3	0.5	0.5	16.5	23.1	20.5
Utilities	0.2	0.2	0.2	5.9	6.8	8.8
Construction	7.6	8.6	7.9	2.9	5.8	5.2
Manufacturing	**28.3**	**28.3**	**26.6**	**3.7**	**5.6**	**4.5**
Wholesale Trade	6.2	6.5	6.5	2.2	4.1	2.7
Retail Trade	9.7	8.6	8.3	-10.2	-7.8	-14.4
Transportation & Warehousing	2.9	3.0	3.0	-1.2	2.7	-1.4
Information	1.3	1.1	1.1	0.9	4.8	2.6
Finance & Insurance	1.2	1.2	1.1	0.6	3.9	2.0
Real Estate and Rental and Leasing	1.1	1.0	0.9	-2.6	1.6	-1.8
Prof., Sci. & Tech. Services	4.2	4.7	5.4	1.9	5.1	3.7
Mgmt. of Companies & Enterprises	0.8	0.8	0.9	5.8	7.6	5.8
Admin., Suppt. & Waste Mgmt.	18.0	18.9	18.6	-12.4	-8.9	-12.2
Educational Services	1.7	1.5	1.6	-28.8	-21.3	-23.4
Health Care & Soc. Assistance	3.1	2.7	3.2	-6.8	-5.5	-7.4
Arts, Entertainment and Recreation	1.1	0.9	1.0	-12.9	-10.1	-17.6
Accommodation & Food Services	6.8	6.4	7.2	-28.9	-24.9	-30.3
Other Services (Excl. Publ. Admin.)	2.4	2.2	2.4	-7.1	-3.6	-6.9
Public Administration*	1.1	1.0	1.1	-4.1	-3.8	-3.0
Manufacturing Flows (thousands)	3374.3	3253.5	2411.6	1406.0	1398.2	1105.6

Notes: Calculated from the set of all job-to-job flows which are within-quarter or in adjacent quarters, in which the origin industry is in the Manufacturing NAICS sector. Manufacturing is in bold for emphasis. Associated median wage changes are available for the subset of job-to-job flows in which both the separation is from and accession is to full-quarter employment, see text for details. Wage changes are calculated for full-quarter earnings of separation job S and accession job A according to (A-S)/((A+S)/2).

*: Public Administration does not include federal workers due to data availability.

Table 9c: Job-to-Job Flows Originating in Finance & Insurance

Destination Industry	Frequency of Destinations			Wage Change (Median)		
	2001-03	2004-06	2007-09	2001-03	2004-06	2007-09
Any Destination Industry	**100.0**	**100.0**	**100.0**	**2.3**	**4.0**	**0.8**
Agric., Forestry, Fishing & Hunting	0.3	0.4	0.5	-6.2	1.3	-7.7
Mining, Quarrying and Gas Extraction	0.1	0.1	0.1	16.7	20.8	18.2
Utilities	0.2	0.1	0.2	10.5	13.9	13.7
Construction	2.1	2.3	2.0	5.4	7.5	5.7
Manufacturing	2.1	2.1	2.0	8.0	10.9	8.3
Wholesale Trade	2.0	2.1	2.3	4.9	8.8	5.4
Retail Trade	7.8	6.9	6.9	-9.3	-6.3	-13.2
Transportation & Warehousing	1.0	1.1	1.1	-2.0	3.1	-1.2
Information	2.5	2.3	2.3	5.0	8.5	7.3
Finance & Insurance	**43.9**	**46.0**	**43.8**	**4.6**	**5.5**	**2.4**
Real Estate and Rental and Leasing	1.9	2.1	1.9	2.7	5.9	0.9
Prof., Sci. & Tech. Services	6.1	6.7	7.5	4.5	7.0	3.6
Mgmt. of Companies & Enterprises	1.5	1.5	1.6	4.3	7.2	4.4
Admin., Suppt. & Waste Mgmt.	11.9	11.5	11.2	-4.9	-2.1	-3.8
Educational Sercvices	2.7	2.4	3.0	-12.7	-7.6	-8.7
Health Care & Soc. Assistance	5.2	4.4	5.2	-0.3	2.0	0.1
Arts, Entertainment and Recreation	1.1	1.0	1.0	-13.5	-8.1	-20.1
Accommodation & Food Services	4.5	4.2	4.4	-28.4	-22.1	-29.3
Other Services (Excl. Publ. Admin.)	1.7	1.6	1.8	-4.9	-1.5	-5.0
Public Administration*	1.4	1.2	1.3	3.6	5.8	5.2
Job-to-Job Flows (thousands)	1365.2	1578.1	1300.0	730.5	870.8	750.4

Notes: Calculated from the set of all job-to-job flows which are within-quarter or in adjacent quarters, in which the origin industry is in the Finance & Insurance NAICS sector. Finance & Insurance is in bold for emphasis. Associated median wage changes are available for the subset of job-to-job flows in which both the separation is from and accession is to full-quarter employment, see text for details. Wage changes are calculated for full-quarter earnings of separation job S and accession job A according to (A-S)/((A+S)/2).

*: Public Administration does not include federal workers due to data availability.

Table 9d: Job-to-Job Flows Originating in Health Care & Soc. Assist.

Destination Industry	Frequency of Destinations			Wage Change (Median)		
	2001-03	2004-06	2007-09	2001-03	2004-06	2007-09
Any Destination Industry	**100.0**	**100.0**	**100.0**	**5.3**	**5.8**	**4.5**
Agric., Forestry, Fishing & Hunting	0.3	0.4	0.4	4.0	5.3	6.8
Mining, Quarrying and Gas Extraction	0.0	0.1	0.1	24.4	41.1	39.6
Utilities	0.1	0.1	0.1	21.6	24.8	26.1
Construction	1.5	1.9	1.8	12.2	13.8	10.6
Manufacturing	2.0	2.1	1.7	18.1	22.5	19.2
Wholesale Trade	1.2	1.3	1.2	12.6	14.6	11.3
Retail Trade	7.5	7.3	6.6	0.0	0.3	-5.5
Transportation & Warehousing	0.9	1.0	0.9	7.5	11.0	7.3
Information	0.8	0.7	0.6	13.5	15.0	14.8
Finance & Insurance	1.8	1.8	1.6	12.0	12.7	11.4
Real Estate and Rental and Leasing	1.2	1.1	1.0	6.8	8.4	6.4
Prof., Sci. & Tech. Services	2.8	2.9	3.0	8.1	10.5	8.1
Mgmt. of Companies & Enterprises	0.6	0.5	0.5	7.8	9.0	9.1
Admin., Suppt. & Waste Mgmt.	11.5	11.6	10.4	1.2	1.5	-1.0
Educational Sercvices	4.8	4.8	4.8	4.5	5.2	5.0
Health Care & Soc. Assistance	**50.7**	**50.3**	**53.1**	**6.1**	**6.2**	**5.6**
Arts, Entertainment and Recreation	1.1	1.0	1.0	0.1	-0.2	-2.4
Accommodation & Food Services	6.5	6.3	6.6	-11.3	-8.1	-9.9
Other Services (Excl. Publ. Admin.)	2.5	2.4	2.6	2.4	4.6	3.8
Public Administration*	2.3	2.6	2.2	11.5	13.1	14.7
Job-to-Job Flows (thousands)	3475.1	3739.1	3392.4	1538.3	1748.0	1668.6

Notes: Calculated from the set of all job-to-job flows which are within-quarter or in adjacent quarters, in which the origin industry is in the Health Care & Social Assistance NAICS sector. Health Care & Social Assistance is in bold for emphasis. Associated median wage changes are available for the subset of job-to-job flows in which both the separation is from and accession is to full-quarter employment, see text for details. Wage changes are calculated for full-quarter earnings of separation job S and accession job A according to (A-S)/((A+S)/2).

*: Public Administration does not include federal workers due to data availability.

www.ingramcontent.com/pod-product-compliance
Lightning Source LLC
Chambersburg PA
CBHW080615180526
45168CB00007B/2929